PHOTOGRAPHY FOR BEGINNERS

From Beginner To Expert Photographer In Less Than a Day!

James Carren

Table of Contents

INTRODUCTION

Many books suggest that the best way to learn to take high-quality photos with your DSLR camera is by randomly taking hundreds of photos and praying that you get a few good ones out of the lot. The books read like stereo instructions, and rarely is the information grouped in a sensible, easy-to-use format. Either the authors assume you are a professional photographer or that you have never seen a camera before. But what about the rest of us who fall somewhere in the middle?

This book was written with a novice to DSLR camera technology in mind. I'm assuming that you have some knowledge of photography, but might have just bought a new DSLR camera and need to know how to use it. Instead of going into abysmal depths on topics like photo imaging and editing software, I've chosen to give you some tips and information. If you decide to expand your knowledge further, feel free to check out my other publications. Furthermore, the internet is also a vast resource for information regarding hardware, software, product reviews, instructions, and even troubleshooting.

I want to give you an idea of how to get out in the field and set your camera (while being aware of the elements in the scene) to take a great photo without a lot of wasted time, effort, and runaround. If you want to know what aperture setting you will need for a particular application, go to the section on apertures. The same thing goes for shutter speed and file formats. It also applies to lighting and other "soft settings" like white balance and exposure. I'll discuss the automatic and manual modes and when it is best to use both of them.

So, is this book an in-depth operator's manual to answer every single question and to cover every possible photographic scenario? No. It's not. Is this book for someone with 30 years of photographic experience? Maybe. If the photographer's experience is with a 35mm film camera and he just bought a new DSLR camera, then, yes, this book would definitely be a good place to start. It discusses how tweaking the settings will affect the resulting photograph.

The book could also be used by someone who has very little experience in photography. There is a lot of jargon in the field and many book authors assume the reader knows what some of the acronyms (like DSLR) and vocabulary mean. I will not make that assumption. I will provide the definition in the text where applicable so you will not have to go flipping through the book to find it. I have tried to organize this book in order of importance for when taking a photograph. The settings may change from subject to subject, but the basic steps will remain the same. And as you become familiar with your camera, many of the steps will become second nature, and you will begin to adjust the settings automatically.

The book also discusses what to do with your photos once you take them. It gives the reader some options and ideas of ways to edit, print, store, share, and display the photos. It also has a chapter discussing how even the most mundane object can become a true piece of art. And I'll explain how everyone's opinion of what constitutes "art" differs. All of these various definitions of "art" are a godsend to photographers because it leaves the door to creativity wide open.

As we all know, people can have very different opinions of what they deem tasteful and aesthetically pleasing. And art comes in all forms, so I encourage you to shoot photos of things, scenes, and people who captivate you. There is more to photography as an art form then just adding photos to the family album, shooting Santa and Easter Bunny pictures at the mall, and photographing flowers. Many times, how you present the images can be construed as art. So, instead of putting them in a box or sharing them on Facebook, maybe you could group them in a unique way to create a collage. The ways to group and organize them are also open to interpretation, so do what moves you. Be brave! Be bold! Try something truly unusual – it may be the next big art movement!

In short, this book is a starting point for anyone wanting a true beginner's guide to DSLR photography. It is by no means an owner's manual. I'll explain terms and discuss the settings and buttons and their functions. And I will discuss how to avoid common problems before you ruin your photos. While practice certainly makes perfect, it does not have to entail wasting time with haphazard shooting and photo editing. Who wouldn't rather learn more quickly and with fewer mishaps than simply learning by trial and error?

CHAPTER 1
THE BIRTH OF DIGITAL PHOTOGRAPHY

A HISTORY OF CAPTURING IMAGES

People have been using different devices to capture images for centuries. The ancient Chinese and Greeks used a simple device called a *camera obscura*, which was nothing more than a light-proof box with a tiny hole in one side, to help them draw images. However, the images formed by the device were only temporary, and they were also upside-down!

It was not until the Middle Ages, circa 1000 AD, when a scientist named Alhazen, originally from modern-day Iraq, created a working prototype of a camera. He accurately described how it worked, and explained why the resulting image was upside-down. Alhazen also described lenses, refraction (how light travels through different materials, thus "bending" rays at different angles), how light can be broken down into colors (the light spectrum), properties of curved mirrors, and various natural phenomena such as shadows, eclipses, rainbows, and spherical aberration (how a single device can bend light at different angles toward its outer edge, blurring the image). Alhazen also studied how the eye works, and directly contradicted the belief of scientists like Euclid and Ptolemy (who believed that the eye emitted its own light rays) by explaining that the eye only receives light and that the image we see is created by the light focusing at the back of the eye.

But, like all things scientific, others took Alhazen's work and expanded it. Refer to the timeline below to see how the simple *camera obscura* mutated into a DSLR.

1826: A French scientist developed a way to temporarily burn an image using the sun.

1837: Another Frenchman developed the *Daguerrotype*, a camera that permanently captured an image on a treated metal plate.

1841: A patent was granted for the process of using negative-positive technology, so people could make multiple copies of the same image.

1844: A German inventor created a camera that could capture panoramic scenes onto a celluloid film.

1861: The first stereoscope viewer was invented; the first photo in permanent color was taken.

1871: The process of using gelatin, dry plate, silver bromide was invented, eliminating the need to process images immediately.

Things really changed in 1880 when the Eastman Dry Plate Company was created. In 1884, George Eastman developed a paper-based film. Then, in 1889, he patented the *Kodak Roll Film Camera*. In 1900, Kodak marketed the first mass-produced camera called "the Brownie," which remained in production until the 1960's.

While Kodak was certainly one of the earliest influences on modern camera technology, the 20th century saw developmental improvements at a dizzying rate. In 1900, the *Raisecamera* came into production and was immediately used by landscape photographers because of the camera's light weight and small size when folded. In 1913-1914, Leica produced the first 35-mm camera. This became the standard by which all film cameras would be judged.

Here is another timeline to highlight the major developments since 1914:

1948: The Polaroid camera was born. Instant photo developing allowed this camera to take a picture, develop it, and print it in about one minute.

1960: The first underwater camera was developed for the U.S. Navy.

1975: Kodak invented the first digital camera.

1980: Sony marketed the very first consumer camcorder.

1981: Sony developed the first digital electronic still camera.

1985: Pixar created the first digital imaging processor.

1986: Fuji released the first disposable camera.

1991: Kodak developed the first professional digital camera.

1994-1996: Many manufacturers developed digital cameras for consumers that worked with their home computers via a cable.

1995: The first websites appeared for sharing digital photos.

2000: Sharp invented a cell phone with a digital camera.

2005: Canon released the first full-framed, DSLR camera with a 24x36 mm CMOS sensor.

WHAT IS SO SPECIAL ABOUT SLR?

Now that you know the history of modern digital cameras, let's look at some differences between them. To understand what makes a SLR camera desirable, you need to know what makes them different from other digital cameras.

For starters, what does "SLR" stand for? It means *single-lens reflex*, or that light is being reflected somewhere else: in this case, to the viewfinder instead of directly to the sensor. There are different possible set-ups inside the camera to achieve this method, whether it is by a pentaprism or fixed mirrors. But, regardless of the set-up, the image is accurately shown in the viewfinder. The mirror in front of the sensor (as explained in a minute) quickly pivots out of the way when you take the picture.

Without using a lot of jargon, this is how the light travels through digital and DSLR cameras. In most digital cameras, the main lens is fixed and it focuses the image directly onto the sensor after passing straight through other elements that will ultimately identify the colors of the image. In SLR, however, the process is a little different.

In SLR cameras, the light travels through the lens and the other elements, but is reflected by a mirror in front of the sensor up into a pentaprism or a set of mirrors, and back to a viewfinder. This accurately shows what the image will look like. When the photo is taken, the mirror moves out of the way so that the image can be received by the sensor. It's a *what-you-see-is-what-you-get* set-up. Also, DSLRs offer removable and replaceable lenses, allowing you to change the lenses to suit your purposes. DSLRs also have a very small lag time, making them ideal for filming action, as well as stills and landscapes. Instead of changing the camera, DSLRs allow you to simply tailor the lens to whatever you are shooting.

Up until recently, DSLRs were only used by professionals or by photographic enthusiasts who could afford the steep costs. But, as with most technology trends, the cost is constantly becoming more reasonable. Now, DSLRs are comparable in price to many high-end digital cameras. This has allowed more people to acquire them. But, because the DSLRs are new to most people, they are not familiar with the features that a DSLR camera offers.

CHAPTER 2
THE MECHANICS OF DSLR—
TWEAKING THE CAMERA SETTINGS

Before launching into how to tweak your camera's settings, we need to discuss a few things. Your specific photography needs will dictate the particular features you buy. Whether you are using this guide to determine which DSLR camera is right for you or if you already own one, this book will help you choose the camera and/or settings that will allow for you to take the best pictures possible.

DSLRs offer a wide array of functions and equipment. I will break down each function and explain what tweaking it can do to your pictures. There are settings for sensitivity, exposure, focus, color modes, white balance, file types, timers, LCD, and even magnification! And because many different features play into each quality aspect, I will list them by specific part. The order here is the same you would use when you set up a shot. This way you don't have to scan the entire book to find out how to set a particular feature.

ISO

ISO is a measure of the light sensitivity of the digital sensor. Digital cameras offer manual settings for ISO including an automatic mode. The best practice is to use the lowest ISO setting possible to reduce the risk of "noise" in your photo. Sensitivity is a relative term dealing with the size of the pixels versus the overall quality of the sensor. A good rule of thumb is to choose a camera with pixels no smaller than 5 microns. If you are shooting fast-action, the ISO can be set higher. In the case of photographing action, a higher ISO will help to increase the shutter speed (which I will discuss further in depth later on).

APERTURE

Aperture is the opening that allows light to enter the camera. The size of the aperture is denoted by an f/stop number. The f/stop number is determined by a ratio of the focal length (f) of a lens to the width of the diaphragm (opening). Basically, it is an inverse proportion: a small aperture is denoted by a higher f/stop number and a large aperture is denoted by a smaller f/stop number. Exposure can be increased with a larger aperture. Aperture settings can also help determine the depth of field (DOF).

Aperture adjustments can also be set automatically. In Aperture Priority mode, you can manually set your aperture and the camera will automatically set the shutter speed.

But, aperture has a definite impact on image quality. You basically want the sharpest details without any annoying visual distortions. An incorrect aperture setting can cause colored halos around objects in the picture (chromatic aberration), darkness at the edges of a photo (vignette), or straight lines to appear bent (pincushion distortion). One way to avoid such distortions is to choose a mid-range aperture. But, different lenses require different apertures. A telephoto lens would need an aperture of f/11 to f/16 (small), but a wide-angle lens would need an aperture of f/5.6 to f/8. A normal lens will mostly use an aperture of f/8 to f/11.

SHUTTER SPEED

Shutter speed is the duration of time light is allowed to hit the sensor. It is calculated by using the reciprocal of the focal length of the lens. For example, a 250mm lens would have a shutter speed of 1/250 second, a 50mm lens would have a shutter speed of 1/60 second, and a 1200mm lens would be best at 1/1000 second shutter speed. There is an automatic mode (Shutter Priority mode) for the shutter as well. If you manually set the shutter speed, the camera will automatically set the appropriate aperture.

Shutter speeds vary with the subject. Shooting a picture of a bowl of fruit requires a slower shutter speed than shooting a hummingbird hovering at a flower. For the hummingbird, slower shutter speeds would cause the wings to look blurry in the image.

Another consideration for photographing anything outdoors is movement caused by the wind. A faster shutter speed may be required to shoot a flower swaying in the breeze. The "noise" described earlier can also be caused by slow shutter speeds.

One thing to be aware of is a slight internal shake from the mirror moving out of the way in DSLR cameras. It is most noticeable at slow shutter speeds, from 1/4 to 1/15 second. A faster shutter speed can offset this slight vibration.

Another feature in DSLRs is a mirror delay function. It is advisable to use the delay feature at shutter speeds of ¼ to 1/30 second. *Please remember to turn this feature off before taking other photos under different settings!!!*

Once you begin using your DSLR camera, these settings will become easier to adjust for your shooting needs. These are the main features that directly impact the quality of your photos, so understanding them is enough to get you started. Your DSLR comes equipped with more features to help you improve the quality, sharpness, color, and contrast. These features also can help reduce or eliminate bothersome visual distortion and noise.

CHAPTER 3
EQUIPMENT AND GEAR

While many built-in features of DSLRs can help you take awesome pictures, there is other equipment that can make your photos even better. These kinds of cameras, as mentioned earlier, have the added bonus of changeable lenses. But, there are also filters, flashes, tripods, computers, and printers to consider. All these elements combine to help you take top-quality photos, but also, to help you process, edit, share, and print them. (The actual software will be discussed in chapter 6.)

There are some basic camera accessories that would help anyone. While there are many options, I will just mention a few. To keep your lenses clean, you will need an optical lens cleaning solution, a lint-free cloth, and a small air blower. A word of caution, though: *do not use cloths pre-treated to clean eyeglasses!* They can damage the coating on your lenses! There are also white balance tools (usually come in the form of cards) which will allow you to set your camera to white, gray, or black. These are used to improve color accuracy.

LENSES

One of the most important decisions you can make for your camera concerns lenses. A lens is a piece of high-quality optical glass that achieves a focus through precise calibration. While DSLRs are only made by a few manufacturers, lenses come from many manufacturers in a wide range of price and quality. There are lenses for all kinds of applications. So, how do you choose a lens? You need to ask yourself a couple questions: *What is my budget?* And *what are my photographic needs?*

The trick is to match the lens to your budget and your purpose. You want the best quality lens that suits your desires and your wallet.

The biggest requirement for any lens, regardless of the purpose, is sharpness. Sharpness equals quality. Not all lenses are consistently sharp across all apertures and fields. You also have to consider the possibility of distortions and noise as described earlier. Are these distortions excessive?

Let me describe the different types of lenses so that you will have an idea about what makes each type unique. A normal, or standard, lens, is usually a lens with a fixed focal length of 35mm, and it captures the realistic proportions of a scene. A wide-angle lens actually shows more width in a scene than is seen by the eyes, so the image may appear to be stretched – this creates a wider field of view. A zoom lens can shoot over a wide range of focal lengths. A telephoto lens almost acts like a telescope: it has a long focal length that magnifies the subject, creating a narrower field of view than is naturally seen with the eyes. A macro lens is designed for high magnification (usually a 1:1 ratio) and extremely close focusing to produce unsurpassed sharpness and detail qualities.

Some basic guidelines about buying lenses will help you get started without forcing you to buy a bunch of unnecessary equipment. The first tip is to buy one high-quality primary lens, one that has a fixed focal length. If you require a zoom lens, confine them to 3x or 4x: 6x and higher zooms seem to have more distortion and a smaller sweet spot for high quality photos. They are also bulkier and often do not equal the quality of simpler zoom lenses.

There are image-stabilized lenses (IS) to help prevent the need for a tripod. While they can prevent some of the blur, it is not a substitute for the stillness of a tripod. At slower shutter speeds, the sharpness with IS lenses will be okay at best. The best results occur when it is used as a normal lens at a shutter speed that is the reciprocal of the focal length or faster. This can achieve impressive sharpness without a tripod. But, you do need to read the instructions. IS lenses do not work at all focal lengths and usually must be set with switches.

But what if you want to shoot something that requires a special lens? There are many types for all situations, so, again, go for the best quality that fits your budget. Each special lens group (these are just some suggestions; it is by no means an exhaustive list) performs best in niche environments which will be briefly described:

If you want to photograph nature, like flowers or very small and detailed subjects, you will most likely require a macro lens that allows very close focusing. The sharpness and detail required for this type of photography far exceed the domain of an all-purpose primary or zoom lens. Many times, a tripod is too cumbersome or even not at all feasible, so an IS lens would be a good choice to help eliminate blur.

If you want to shoot photos of your child's football game, you need a lens that can perform in different lighting and over different aperture fields. You will require a fast-focus telephoto lens that will take sharp photo of a brilliant flying tackle on a sunny day, or of a quarterback sack in dim evening light.

What about photographing large buildings like cathedrals or monuments? A normal lens or a wide-angle lens can drastically distort and unnaturally bend the lines in the architecture. For this type of photography, a shift lens will provide an accurate perspective (with straight lines) of a building.

Many amateur photographers ask about the best type of lens to use while filming important events, like weddings or christenings. Many times, these scenes are wide and the subjects can change quickly. In churches, the light is fairly dim, so sharpness is critical in capturing the bride's dazzling gown and the delicate hues and textures of the flower bouquets. For most applications, a fast moderate to wide-angle telephoto lens will perform reasonably well under the constraints of the job. However, IS lenses may also be useful here to prevent any undesirable blurring.

If you want to take photographs of a lone tree in the middle of a corn field or of the Grand Canyon, landscape photography requires a wide-angle lens that offers razor-sharp clarity from edge to edge. It should maintain the sharpness even at small apertures. You want details to be sharp across the image, with the least amount of light falling-off (also known as vignetting, or the unusual patterns that shows up in dark areas of a photo) or flaring (which can appear as light-colored shapes in the viewfinder and/or the image).

If you do use a zoom lens, for reasons stated earlier, be sure that it is less than a 6x zoom. One issue to be aware of is zoom creep. This sometimes happens when using long exposure times. The zoom collar can slip through the entire range of focal lengths during the shot! The result is a blurry image. Some zoom lenses actually have a zoom lock that addresses this issue.

Four-thirds (4/3) lenses are usually specific to the camera manufacturer and are designed for the requirements of the sensor, not of film, making them smaller and better-performing than lenses built for film. They actually send light perpendicular to the pixel buckets, reducing the chance that some light will miss the pixel buckets.

FILTERS

In the days of 35mm film cameras, photographers needed an arsenal of filters for different effects: some were to block out unwanted light and some were to protect the lens from ultraviolet (UV) light. But, with the advent of image-editing software like Adobe® and Photoshop®, the need for filters has decreased drastically. However, here are a few suggestions for filters that may come in handy or eliminate the need for editing work later:

- A UV filter will protect your lens.
- A neutral-density filter will reduce light and allow the use of faster shutter speeds or larger apertures.
- A graduated neutral-density filter will balance a brilliantly vivid sky with a darker foreground.
- A polarizing filter will reduce reflections from shiny surfaces and can make white clouds really stand out in the sky.

FLASHES

There are all different types of flashes: some are built-in and while others do not even touch your camera. They are all used for specific effects by applying a flash of light in some fashion to the scene. Flashes allow photographers to take excellent photos in almost any light.

Most DSLRs have an on-board pop-up flash as a standard feature. The light is sent directly to the subject, often resulting in too-bright subjects against a too-dark background. But, DSLRs also have a way to meter the ambient light and balance the flash accordingly to avoid these garish contrasts.

A dedicated flash is an external flash that snaps into your DSLRs hot shoe (a slot on top of the camera). It actually uses the camera settings of aperture, ISO, f/stop number, shutter speed, and lens length to customize the light flash. Many dedicated flashes have a pre-flash that allows subjects' eyes to constrict properly, effectively eliminating red-eye. Some dedicated flashes even come with a cable that allows the flash to be held away from the camera at any angle.

For extreme close-up photography requiring macro lenses, there is a ring-light flash that screws onto the lens attachment threads. It offers a soft, diffused light that brings out details while eliminating harsh contrast and shadows.

Attaching to the tripod bushings is another flash: the hammerhead flash. This stays separate from the camera. It offers a bright output at an off-axis angle that limits red-eye. It is used widely for weddings and among the media.

TRIPOD

While built-in image stabilization, IS lenses, and resting your arms on a stationary object will help to improve the sharpness of your photos, they cannot top the stabilization of a tripod.

As usual, the same considerations come into play: which tripod is best for me? And what is my budget?

There are other considerations as well. You must not only read the specifications, but try the tripod out for yourself. You must think about the weight of the tripod, stability, the maximum camera weight it can support, the tripod head (is it interchangeable?), camera orientation, leg extensions, overall height, and all its possible configurations. The tripod must match your needs. You do not want to buy a behemoth tripod that can extend to 6 ft tall if you are using it to take photos of your mother's chrysanthemum beds.

Also, keep in mind that the tripod head needs to hold your camera very steady, even while using your largest and heaviest lens. How quickly do you want to set it up? Some have adapters to address speed and ease of setup. Do the legs extend smoothly, lock, or buckle? Is it light enough to reasonably carry?

All those questions will determine the tripod that is right for you. Depending on your particular photography needs, there may be other questions to consider as well. It's best to answer them honestly so that you get the most use out of your tripod.

COMPUTER AND PRINTER

Although computer technology changes almost weekly, the choice of computer system, whether desktop or laptop, will be determined by your needs and your wallet. For comparable systems, a laptop will cost about 1/3 more than a desktop. Also, laptops are not as versatile about adding memory, video cards, etc. But, whichever system you choose, it needs speed and power if you plan to use it for photo processing and editing.

You will also want a high-quality monitor to accurately view your images. Sizes larger than 19-in are best. While CRT monitors delivered excellent color accuracy and were easily calibrated, they are now quickly giving way in favor of lighter, thinner LCD (Liquid Crystal Display) monitors. But, either way, your monitor will probably need to be calibrated if you want to see true-to-life color accuracy. Why? Have you ever gone to a store selling televisions? Not a single screen shows the same colors! The same thing happens with monitors. But, calibration can easily be done with software specifically designed for this purpose.

If you plan on printing your photos, you really can't go wrong in buying a higher-end inkjet photo printer. Epson claims they are unsurpassed in quality. With printers, not only are there the usual considerations of needs and budget, but also that of ink and paper. As a rule of thumb, pigment inks last longer than dye inks. Make sure your printer can handle the type of ink you wish to use. It is advisable to purchase ink from the same manufacturer who makes your printer.

Also consider the size. Prints can be made from wallet-sized to wall-sized: how big of a sheet of paper do you want your printer to handle? There is also a dazzling array of quality photo paper available – from printer manufacturers like Epson and HP, to independent paper companies.

Printers also use different technologies to apply the ink to the paper (Epson uses piezo while HP and Canon use thermal). Piezo technology uses an electrical current to change the shape of a crystal housed in the ink head to allow a drop of ink to escape. Thus, the ink is not heated and the size of the ink droplets can be very small. Thermal (or bubble jet, as it is commonly called) technology also uses an electrical current. But, in thermal printers, the current is applied to a small resistor housed in the ink head. The resistor heats up and boils a tiny bit of ink that can then squeeze out. The ink in these printers must withstand temperatures of up to 1000°F! This temperature requirement eliminates many chemicals and inks. But, any differences in quality between photos made with these technologies will be negligible for most purposes.

CHAPTER 4
TAKING THE BEST PICTURE POSSIBLE—LIGHTING, SETTING, FOCUS

Now that you are aware of some of the settings on your camera, there are other aspects to consider. Many other properties will be just as important to the quality and aesthetic beauty of your photos. This chapter will break these other elements down. They are not hard settings, per se, but do allow for flexibility where needed.

FILE FORMAT

When you decide to take a picture, you not only have to tweak your camera's physical settings, you have a host of other settings, too. One setting is the file format you want your photo to be recorded in. The most common formats are JPEG, TIFF, and RAW. To choose the format that is right for you, you need to know what each format offers and what its limitations are.

JPEGs (Joint Photographic Experts Group) pretty much work with any computer and any photo editing software.

They are an 8-bit format that scans each image for redundancy and automatically eliminates it. And this compresses the files. If you edit a JPEG file, you are actually editing the pixels, and degrading the quality of the image. However, if you set the camera to record in the highest resolution with the least amount of compression, the resulting JPEG image will be very high quality. JPEGs also provide another file containing information about the camera settings like white balance, tonal adjustment, sharpening, and saturation. But, if you want to work with your photos in editing software, save them in a non-compressing format like TIFF.

Speaking of TIFF (Tagged Image File Format), if you want to edit your photos, TIFF does not compress the file, nor does it destroy data. It is a popular format that will, again, work with most computers and photo editing software. It is also an 8-bit file format.

Then, there is RAW. RAW is a file format that is specific to a camera manufacturer. It is a 12-bit format and does no processing to the image: all of the processing is done with software. But, the RAW file records more than just the image: it also records your camera's "soft settings," like white balance, resolution, color mode, saturation, and contrast. When you edit a RAW file, you only make different versions of the original image – the pixel data is not altered, damaged, or destroyed. A camera manufacturer's RAW editing software cannot open a competitor's RAW file. However, third-party editing software like Photoshop® Camera

RAW can open and edit RAW files from most camera manufacturers.

There is also a setting for RAW+JPEG. This preserves all the information for both formats.

LIGHTING

One of the most critical aspects of photography is lighting. The right lighting can produce a spectacular photo, while the wrong lighting makes one that are too bright with too few details or too dark with lots of noise. So, how do you know what to do?

There are two purposes to consider with lighting: creating the amount of detail sharpness you desire and making a workable tonal range. Tonal range will be mentioned again in the exposure section.

Of course, it is much easier to control and manipulate lighting indoors. You can use fill lights to lighten shadowy areas (reducing the risk of noise) and light blockers or filters to darken highlights to sharply bring out the details.

Outdoor photography, on the other hand, offers a host of obstacles to lighting. Sometimes the sun will blind you, throwing out a lot of glare. Sometimes, it is so cloudy, that it appears to be twilight. And what if you shoot something that has sun and shadows? How can you account for all the variations of light? In reality, there is only so much you can do.

If you are shooting somewhere with lots of reflected light, filters may help dampen and even out the image. If there is just too much light, photos may be taken in a broad range of exposures. Sometimes, you may have to shoot the subject from a different angle to capture more detail. And what of the sun and shadows scenario? A photographer can use fill lights to reduce that harsh contrast in lighting under those conditions. If none of those options give you the detail and sharpness you want, it may be necessary to simply wait until the lighting is more favorable!

COLOR MODES AND WHITE BALANCE

There are manual and automatic settings on your camera that can determine the way color is recorded and how true those colors will be. The first is the color mode. Most digital cameras offer a choice in color modes.

The modes are Adobe RBG, sRBG, or ProPhoto RBG. sRBG was designed to be displayed on color monitors and to be used on the internet. It has the smallest color range of the three types. But, many print shops and printers are set up to use sRBG files, so it's easy to find printing equipment that can handle the files. Adobe RBG has a wider color range for discrete colors. Because camera equipment is evolving, printing equipment is also evolving to handle the more sophisticated Adobe RBG files. ProPhoto RBG has an even wider color range and can handle more manipulation in the image processing software.

Regardless of which color mode you select, a JPEG file will apply those settings to the image. But, if you shoot a RAW image, the color mode does not matter because you can select the mode later on when you process it with the RAW software.

So, what is white balance, then? White balance is basically a setting that assigns a temperature value (in Kelvin, K) to a light source. Mid-day sunshine is about 5500K, and it displays all the red, blue, and green (RBG) colors in equal amounts, giving off what we call "white light." But, you won't always take photos in the sunshine at noon, so you'll have to adjust the white balance to retain accurate colors in the photos.

Your camera has an automatic setting mode for white balance and the results are usually fine. However, if you want very consistent results, it would be wise to consider manually setting the white balance to the current lighting situation. One way to do this is to place a white card in the photo to be used by the processing software later. Or, you can make a custom white balance procedure that can be used anytime, regardless of the lighting.

To create a custom procedure, you will want to use a card of white, gray, or an Expodisc. Adjust the card so that it receives the same lighting as your subject. Focus on the white balance tool on your camera and press the shutter button. But, check your camera's owner manual to ensure that this procedure will accurately set the white balance.

If you are using the RAW format, the software adjusts the white balance when you process the file. So, should you even bother fiddling with the white balance when you try to shoot a photo? Consider your format: are you taking RAW files or RAW+JPEG? It is usually a good practice, regardless, to go ahead and set the white balance before you even take the photo. It will save you time when you process it.

SETTING, CAMERA POSITION, COMPOSITIONAL BRACKETING

The compositional subject of your photos is entirely up to you. On a hike, you may want to take photos of different things in the same location. For example, in the Great Smoky Mountains, you may want to take a panoramic shot from the trail to show the hazy, tree-covered mountains off in the distance. But, at the same location, there are huge rhododendron bushes you would also like to photograph. You obviously want a different camera position and lenses for each shot. While we like to think that the subject always needs to be dead-center in the photograph, these images may not exactly be artistic or interesting. Adding tilts to your shots can increase the aesthetic value in some cases.

So, what are some basic tips on camera position and bracketing to create the ultimate photos? There are a few things to consider when talking about camera placement.

The single, largest impact of camera placement is on the lighting in the scene. Depending on the camera location, you can highlight, emphasize, lighten, darken, hide, or minimize individual elements in a scene. It is a matter of choice for how you wish to use the camera's perspective and resultant light and shadows.

If you are not concerned with a depth of field and you only want very sharp detail, then you will want to shoot the subject directly, making the angle of your line of sight at a 90˚ angle to the subject (perpendicular). The image will probably not have a lot of light or shadow contrasts, but the details will be brilliantly highlighted!

However, if you are shooting outside, there is a good chance that light and shadows will come into play. The camera angle and the lens choices can create high-contrast scenes. Sometimes, it may be necessary to add some fill lights to brighten up the dark areas to bring out details, but, sometimes, you may want to leave the darkness as-is for a stark, dramatic effect.

Also, if you want to shoot portraits, or any photos of people, be mindful that the combination of camera angle and lighting can have dramatic effects on the resulting photo. Be aware that the main focal points on a face, like the eyes, nose, forehead, and chin can become grotesque if photographed in the wrong lighting or at certain camera angles. While you may enjoy the visual effect, your subject may think the effect is far from flattering!

Whatever you choose to photograph and from whichever angle, you want to compose the shot so that you will not have to crop much later. If you crop in-camera, you can take a shot that uses most of your camera's pixels. However, if you take a shot that requires cropping during processing, yes, the image will be enlarged, but so will all the flaws and noise in the original image. Cropping also reduces the number of pixels you will ultimately use, reducing the overall quality of your photo. So, it is best to take a photo that needs little-to-no cropping during processing to preserve the quality of the image.

FOCUSING AND DEPTH OF FIELD

No amount of image processing software can help a photo that is out of focus. Focus is critical to any image. The trick is to determine what to focus on. This will change drastically from subject to subject, and even from photo to photo.

Focus also brings out the depth of field of a photo. A depth of field (DOF) is the area in front of and behind the plane of focus where all details are sharp. DOF can be as large as miles, or as small as millimeters.

Your camera comes with many settings for autofocus. Some of the autofocus modes are for action photography and are designed to focus much faster than you can when the timing is critical. There is also a single-area autofocus that may have a focus lock. Or, there are manual focus modes for selecting the right focus for close-up photography. This is commonly used in nature photography. Often, in nature photography, a telephoto lens with a large aperture is used. This can focus sharply on the most minute detail, and, incidentally, often have tiny DOFs as well.

It is worth mentioning here that, sometimes, having things out of focus in the background can be a good thing. First, it can highlight and emphasize whatever is in the foreground while leaving the background a pleasing blur, more for artistic or aesthetic effect. Secondly, in the Japanese art of Bokeh, a sharply-focused subject is emphasized by a very out-of-focus background. Bokeh has taken nature and sports photography by storm. In fact, I personally see it in use by photographers shooting bullfights in Portugal: the bull and bullfighter are in sharp focus (showing kicked-up dirt and hair on the bull's nose) while the wall and crowd in the background are a blur of soft shapes and pretty colors. Even some lens manufacturers are creating lenses with a Bokeh assessment in mind.

So, how do we actually determine the DOF? It is not an easy question to answer because not all DSLRs and lenses come with the same information. Many DSLRs have a DOF button that shows what the image will look like in the viewfinder. While it can be a handy tool, it may not be easy to tell the edge to edge sharpness in the image because the viewfinder is so small. Also, at small apertures, like f/11 and f/16, the images in the viewfinder are too dark to view accurately. So, how can you determine DOF manually?

Many zoom lenses have some form of DOF tables for referral. All you have to do is to find and set the focal distance. Some lenses have scales, but depending on the size of the DSLR sensor, the distances may be off. There are ways of using your camera's lens multiplier to determine DOF and the required aperture setting. If, for some reason, your camera does not allow enough DOF for your needs, you may be able to overlay two images:

one closer in and one farther away (both in focus) with your image processing software.

EXPOSURE

Exposure can make or break your photos. It can be the difference between a mediocre shot and an amazing shot. Exposure determines the tones, colors, highlights, shadows, and details in the image. Basically, if your photo is exposed incorrectly, the quality will be reduced.

Exposure is achieved differently with DSLRs than it was with older technology. Before meters, photographers guessed at the correct exposure. Meters helped, but there was still no way to be sure until you took the photo and processed it. A digital camera's built-in meter will survey your shot and adjust for an exposure. But, DSLRs also have a histogram that displays the tonal RBG values of your image. It tells if your exposure is on-target, underexposed, or overexposed. The combination of meter and histogram may not ensure perfect exposure every time, but that may be a good thing. Sometimes, creative or dramatic effect may dictate over or underexposure, but it is a matter of aesthetics and taste.

While the histogram assigns the tonal values to the reds, blues, and greens, the meter sees the image as a series of mid-tones, or grays. Meters determine the exposure by analyzing the image's mid-tones as compared to the aperture setting and shutter speed.

While neither method is perfect, they are invaluable tools in determining the proper exposure. Many books will tell you to take lots of photos first to become acquainted with how the meter and histogram work. Unfortunately, many of those random "first shots" will be thrown out. I think that is a waste of time and energy. The best approach is to learn as much as you can about your camera's settings, make notes, and then apply the notes to take a few shots. If you did your homework right, there will be little wasted time and few trashed photos!

CHAPTER 5
WHAT TO DO WITH YOUR PHOTOS?

As described earlier, the first thing you need to do is get the pictures off of your camera. Depending upon the file format you used, and your skill level, you may have to edit the photos. There are many types of photo editing software available for JPEG, TIFF, and RAW files. Each software has its strengths and weaknesses, so your best bet would be to read product reviews and choose the software that best suits your needs.

We already discussed how to take the best photos possible with your DSLR. We also discussed camera settings and camera placements, angles, lighting, and how built-in features can help you improve the quality of your photos. There is software available that can also help to make these photos even better.

Some of the image processing software can correct color, white balance, and exposure. We also mentioned the hardware you may need (like computers and printers) to process and print your photos.

But what happens when some of those photos are less-than-perfect? Can software fix most problems? What types of images can be salvaged? What needs to be thrown in the trash? Some photos are doomed, regardless of your Photoshop skills. If you have images with these fatal flaws, no amount of editing will help if you want top-quality photos:

- Blur. It does not matter how or why the image blurred, the photo is doomed. No software can correct it.
- Poor composition requiring severe cropping. Every percentage of crop reduces the quality of the image. Severe cropping will seriously degrade the subject unless you do not mind making the subject into a very small print without enlarging it.
- JPEGs with mediocre quality or severe color issues should be trashed because JPEG compression deletes data and there may be serious quality problems that Photoshop cannot hide or repair.
- Photos that are severely over- or underexposed are also doomed. Photoshop may be able to help some, but the quality will be less-than-stellar and the image still may be irreparable.

So, you have sorted your photos and have saved the best ones. Now what? You have all these fabulous photos and you have lots of choices about what to do with them. You can save them, print them, share them, or all of the above!

Saving image files is always a good practice as a back-up and storage plan. No matter what else you do with them, you will want to save them. In the technological world we live in today, you can save them on your Cloud, online in vaults, on external hard drives, on memory sticks, or even on your home computer. So, after all the work it took to get the images, make sure to save them via the method(s) that best suit your needs.

Printing offers options as well. There are photo print shops that specialize in making high-quality prints from image files. You can even audition print shops to check their quality. Many print shops will allow you to choose the type of paper: inkjet or silver halide. Silver halide is traditional photo paper redesigned to work for digital photographs. The quality is comparable to inkjet paper, but the choices for surfaces and textures are more limited. And if you do not want to trust your prized memories with a photo printing shop? Print them yourself.

Manufacturers are now designing printer ink and paper to work together to last as long as possible. A traditional type of paper for documents and photos in the past was archival paper. Archival paper is still used for this purpose if you are already familiar with it. Now, however, there are many other types of paper that withstand the test of time as well.

But, there are more issues for photos than just time. The paper and ink also react with the environment. So, proper storage is essential if you want to preserve the integrity of your photos.

The tips for proper storage of printed paper photos are fairly straightforward:

- Store your photos in acid-free boxes or other containers designed to store photographs.
- Place photographs in the dark to prevent the ink from fading in the sunlight.
- Store photos in a relatively dry environment, between 30 and 50% humidity.
- Store photos away from gases like ozone that can fade photos and degrade ink.

Once you print your images, you can look at them under full-spectrum lamps that have become popular in recent years. This will show how accurate the colors are under natural white light. While mid-day sun is about 5500K, many of the natural light lamps are about 6500K. You can make any adjustments in your editing software if the printed image is not what you wanted.

After you have your prints, either from your own printer or from a photo printing lab, it is time to store them or to display them. Storage suggestions above will keep your prints vivid and bright for many years. But what if you want to display them?

The practice of placing diplomas and important documents under glass serve the same purpose here: to protect the ink and paper from the environment while they are on display. Whether your photographs are properly stored or displayed, they should last for many years.

But what about those digital images still on your computer or stored in memory somewhere? What if you want to share them? It is much easier, actually, to share a digital photo than it is to share one that has been printed already. With the advent of the internet, in a couple clicks, your picture can be seen by thousands of people, almost instantly. There are literally millions of sites available for sharing photos of all kinds. Some of these will be listed by type in the next chapter. So, you can share pictures with your family, or with the world; the internet lets you do it all!

CHAPTER 6
SEEING THE WORLD FROM BEHIND A LENS

Once you learn how to use your DSLR camera, you now need to go out and take amazing photos. But for what purpose? Are you taking photos for your family albums? Are you an avid scrapbooker and need lots of fun photos? Are you a photographer for a paper or magazine, or do you work for other types of media? Are you a blogger or web designer who needs content photos for your websites? Are you a business owner needing to take photos of your products? Are you an avid sports fan or naturist? Do you love taking portraits? Are you a wedding or special event photographer? Do you document your travels (or daily walks) with photos taken on the fly?

What do you like to photograph? Your kids? Your family? Your pets? Animals in general? Flowers? Birds? Trees? Gardens? Beaches? Landscapes? Buildings? Random things you see, like an old abandoned barn sitting in an overgrown field (because there was a tin Coke sign and a rusty tractor in the doorway)? In short, you shoot what you like and what captures your attention.

Whatever your reasons for taking photos, you need to know what subject to photograph. That may not always be obvious. And what about the photos themselves? What do you plan to do with them? Many times, we have a specific purpose in mind when we buy a nice camera to take photos. But, if you are like me, that original purpose may change at any moment!

All of this begs the question of "why?" If I saw the trees blooming in my grandma's yard, I'd whip out my camera to get different types of shots: farther away, grouped in a composition, or close-ups of the blossoms. These photos have sentimental value for me, but some would consider them "art." In any library or bookstore, go peruse a book on art. What are the subjects? Do you consider everything you see in the books as art? I certainly do not.

We all see the world through a different set of eyes. What I see as a bumblebee lazily hovering over the holly bushes may make some scream in horror: our perspectives are totally different. It goes back to the old saying that beauty is in the eye of the beholder... or in this case, the camera holder. Also, quality is sometimes quite subjective as well. Someone may think bold splashes of color is high-quality art, while others think it is total rubbish. Art has even been known to offend some people, while still others love it. Everyone has a different opinion of what counts as "art."

So, what do you do? Exactly what you want. If you want to photograph your neighbor's gnome collection to make a collage for the local garden center, then go for it!

Will everyone go gaga over it? Probably not. But, most will probably think it has interest merit, if nothing else. This goes to show that nearly any subject can create a beautiful photograph. And who knows what a pile of photographs can become. There is no limit to the possibilities when you allow your imagination to run free.

The possibilities are endless. The subjects are endless. If you want to share your objects of beauty (your photos) with the world, the internet is your playground. Book publishers and magazine publishers are becoming increasingly aware of the power of niche photography, like crafts, textures, backgrounds, nature, landscapes, sporting events, etc. The list goes on and on.

The best thing to do is to keep your camera handy. You never know when something is going to call you to photograph it. And do not be shy in sharing your photos. There are the usual social media sites, of course, but there are lots of other sites as well. Flickr and Shutterbug are two that immediately jump to mind. Many proprietary and fan websites invite members to share pertinent photos. Crafting sites like Etsy and Pinterest have become havens for photographers – on more topics than I could begin to list.

The world is full of possible subjects, and there are many outlets for printing, sharing, and selling your photos. All you need to do is to get started. This book will help you to do just that.

CONCLUSION

Now that you have a basic knowledge and plenty of tips to add to your photographer's tool belt, you are ready to begin shooting fabulous photos! Once you capture your images, you have plenty of other options for what to do with them.

Use this book as a general reference guide and as a way to test the waters of DSLR photography without investing a lot of time and money unnecessarily. You'll be able to determine what you need and what you want after reading this book. You will be able to expand your equipment as your interests dictate. And, most importantly, when the scrutiny is off the technique, you can have some fun with it.

After all, photography is not all nuts, bolts, knobs, lights, switches, apertures, and shutter speeds, right? If you are a diehard photography fan, go make your own *camera obscura*: wow your friends with the images you make from a simple box. (I used an International Coffee container!) Find a way to include friends and family, and that can be more than simply being the subjects. It's fun to be a part of any photography process. Use creepy lighting and obtuse camera angles to make scary Halloween photos, then laminate them and use them on a gravestone in your haunted cemetery. Make scary collages for a party. Cut them out and make masks. Use the holidays for inspiration.

Allow your creativity to prevail. Sure, you can post your photos to the web, create stunning displays, make fun scrapbooks. Keeping the fun in the art will allow you (and your family) to enjoy it for many years to come. Plus, if you have children or grandchildren, what better gift to pass on than the love of photography?

Surely, as technology evolves and advances, this book, like your DSLR camera may go into the scrap heap, but the love of capturing images dates back to ancient times. We all have our own agendas when it comes to photography, but at least one of those reasons should include passing something down to the next generation, no? Even if it is merely a fascination with technology or an appreciation for all things beautiful and creative, share your love of photography with the world. You never know what can happen and who your art will speak to!

DID YOU LIKE "PHOTOGRAPHY FOR BEGINNERS"?

Before you go, I'd like to say thank you so much for purchasing my book.

I know you could have picked from dozens of books on this subject, but you took a chance with mine, and I'm truly grateful for that.

So, once again, a big thanks for downloading this book and reading all the way to the end—I truly appreciate it.

Now I'd like to ask for a small favor if you don't mind:

Would you be so kind as to take a minute of your time and leave a review for this book on Amazon?

This feedback will help me continue to write the kind of books that help you get results. And if you loved it, then please feel free to let me know!
:)

MORE BOOKS BY JAMES CARREN

Portrait Photography - 9 Tips Your Camera Manual Never Told You About Portrait Photography

Landscape Photography - 10 Essential Tips to Take Your Landscape Photography to The Next Level

Photography Lighting - Top 10 Must-Know Photography Lighting Facts to Shoot Like a Pro in Your Home Studio

Photography Business: 20 Things You Need to Know Before Starting a Successful Photography Business